j599.2 Rue, Leonard Lee.
RUE
     Meet the opossum

DATE			

Meet the Opossum

Meet the Opossum

LEONARD LEE RUE III
with William Owen

Illustrated with photographs by Leonard Lee Rue III

DODD, MEAD & COMPANY • NEW YORK

*To Harry Schnieber, my teacher, my friend, with whom
I have traveled many miles—L.L.R.*

*To my children Aaron and Leah whose love of animals
is especially nocturnal—W.O.*

All photographs © Leonard Lee Rue III
Drawings on page 19 by Kendel Knouse Culton

Copyright © 1983 by Leonard Lee Rue III and William Owen
All rights reserved
No part of this book may be reproduced in any form
without permission in writing from the publisher
Distributed in Canada by
McClelland and Stewart Limited, Toronto
Manufactured in the United States of America

1 2 3 4 5 6 7 8 9 10

Library of Congress Cataloging in Publication Data

Rue, Leonard Lee.
    Meet the opossum.

    Includes index.
    Summary: Discusses the physical characteristics,
behavior, habitat, food habits, and babies of a
mammal that has inhabited the Earth since the time of
the giant dinosaurs.
    1. Opossums—Juvenile literature. [1. Opossums]
I. Owen, William, 1942–   II. Title.
QL737.M34R84 1983   599.2   83-14033
ISBN 0-396-08221-1

Contents

Preface

I first became acquainted with wild animals while growing up on our farm in northern New Jersey near the Delaware Water Gap. I began taking pictures of them, and it was during those years before my teens that I learned patience. I would sit for hours with my Brownie box camera in a field, waiting for the white-tailed deer to come, hoping that they would arrive before there was too little light left for a good exposure. However, deer were comparatively easy to photograph. The beaver, fox, woodchuck, and opossum were far more difficult. Birds were no problem because they would come to a feeder placed outside my window and would get used to me and my camera inside the glass.

It was an exciting time—observing animals, learning about them, and photographing them. It became more than a pastime or hobby, of course. Today it is my work and my life. The learning process was gradual and satisfying and taught me to respect and cherish nature and her wild-life. I have often wished I had been born several hundred years ago when I could have seen the real wilderness and its multitudes of creatures. However, I am thankful that at least I was born into the present time to be able to see the remnants of our wildlife and to have the opportunity to photograph them.

The opossum is a favorite animal of mine because it seems so dumb and helpless, but has managed to survive on earth for millions of years. As a boy, I remember opossums always wandering into my traps, and how easy it was to catch one by the tail. I wouldn't advise you to try that little trick, though, because a possum will curl up quick as a wink and bite your hand.

Over the years I have captured many of these remarkable animals and observed and photographed them at various stages. I have raised families of opossums and studied their ways. The photographs of baby opossums here were taken of babies that were found in road-killed mothers. I would never sacrifice an animal for the sake of investigation or study. The other photographs were taken over a period of years. I hope you will be as fascinated as I have been with one of nature's real survivors, the opossum.

—Leonard Lee Rue III

1

Meet the Opossum

The opossum has been around for millions of years, making it one of our oldest living mammals—animals that nourish their young with milk. It inhabited the earth at the time of the giant dinosaurs. Fossil remains of marsupials—pouched mammals—have revealed their presence over a hundred million years ago. Now the brontosaurus is gone, the ferocious sabre-toothed tiger has disappeared, and the speedy eohippus, the earliest horse, has vanished. They are extinct, and yet the opossum survives. Let's find out about this little creature that has outlasted so many larger ones.

The opossum is a marsupial, a mammal that carries its young in a pouch called a *marsupium*. The common opossum is found no where else in the world except North America, specifically in the United States. It is the only marsupial in this country. The reason for this is not conclusively known. Eons ago there were many more marsupials on earth. Today they are found only in Australia and nearby islands and in North and South America. Somewhere along the way, they were unable to adjust to changing conditions.

The common opossum of North America has cousins in Mexico and in Central and South America. There is the mouselike murine opossum that is less than two inches in length and resembles a mouse in appearance. The shrew opossum of Brazil is less than three inches long and, as the name indicates, is like a shrew, with short legs and tail, a pointed snout, and tiny eyes. The water opossum or yapok is native to the jungles of South America and is the only marsupial adapted to partly aquatic life. The woolly opossum also lives in tropical South America and is appropriately named, since it has dense fur and its tail is furred at the base. There is a four-eyed opossum in Central America. It does not really have four eyes, but has two white spots surrounded by black coloring just above the eyes. These spots are protective, confusing predators and deterring them from striking the real eyes.

You have to go to Australia and nearby islands in the South Pacific to find other marsupials—kangaroos, wallabies, Tasmanian devils, tiny pouched mice, wombats. But let's get back to our own marsupial, the opossum of North America.

The opossum's scientific family name is Didelphidae. All females of opossum species native to the Americas have two wombs, and the name comes from Greek words—*di* for double and *delphys* for womb. Such marsupials are called Didelphids.

The opossum is the only marsupial in the United States.

"Opossum" is an Indian name. This is a male opossum.

The opossum of North America is known as *Didelphis marsupialis. D. marsupialis virginiana* is the common variety found in the eastern United States and the one that is the subject of this book. Indians gave the animal its name "opossum," and Captain John Smith of the Jamestown colony, who was one of the first Englishmen ever to see a Didelphid, carried the name back to Europe.

The Indians, as far as I can discover, had little use for the opossum. Its fur is of inferior quality and its meat was not to their liking.

The Indians did tell tales of this unusual animal, mostly to explain its queer habits and characteristics. There are

Southeastern Indian stories of how the opossum received its pouch, why the opossum has no hair on its tail, and why the opossum drools and grins. They are all stories that indicate the Indians' curiosity about the opossum. As a child, I often wondered "why," as the Indians must have. With the help of observation, science, and a camera, I had most of my questions answered. The common opossum has proven to be a most interesting animal worthy of our study.

2

Picture a Possum

The opossum is a house cat-sized mammal that resembles a silver rat. This impression is given by its naked ears, its long scaly tail, and its silver-tipped fur.

An adult male opossum may measure up to 40 inches in length, of which the tail is 12 to 15 inches. Weights average six to seven pounds for the adult male and four to five pounds for the fully grown female. William Hamilton, Professor of Mammalogy at Cornell University, recorded the heaviest male he weighed at 11 pounds 2 ounces, and the heaviest female at 7 pounds 4 ounces. One wild opossum was recorded at 14 pounds. A tame opossum owned by a man in Clauton, Alabama, weighed 35 pounds.

The northern opossums are slightly heavier than their southern counterparts, until late fall when winter sets in. After November the southern opossums will weigh more, as they are more active while those in the north are forced to den up. The males are more stocky and chunkier than the females.

An opossum's face is almost pure white, its nose is pink, its ears are hairless.

The face of the opossum is almost pure white, the nose is pink, and the eyes are like black shoe buttons. The ears have a soft, leathery feeling, are hairless, and are black with the top quarter white. There are four rows of whiskers (*vibrissae*) that are about three inches in length. These whiskers are touch sensitive and enable the opossum to avoid collision with solid objects in its path.

The longer hairs poking through the fur on an opossum's back are protective guard hairs that keep the undercoat from becoming worn. They are two and a quarter inches long and are pure white. The undercoat hair is one and a quarter inches long, kinky and white with black tips. The white guard hairs sticking up through the dark hairs give the opossum its silver-grizzled coloration. There is a darker streak down the middle of the back.

On the opossum's belly the guard hairs are almost completely absent; those that are there are short. The undercoat there is about one-half inch in length, sparse and almost white. The fur on the opossum's legs is black.

Albinism (all-white animals) is quite common in the opossum. Melanism (all-black animals) occurs sometimes, and some opossums appear to be reddish-brown. The male opossum has a large gland beneath its chin that oozes a liquid that stains its chest yellow. I have discovered no purpose for this gland. Perhaps it serves to mark a territory or has an odor that attracts the female or discourages enemies.

There is no apparent molting of the opossum's winter coat as in many other animals. The hairs are shed individually.

The opossum's scaly tail is prehensile, making it the only animal in North America that can use its tail for grasping. "Prehensile" means being able to wrap around and grab objects, and the opossum uses its tail like a fifth hand.

A grown opossum is the size of a house cat, but looks more like a silver rat.

The scales of the tail are an off-white color and it is hairless. There are some stiff, short bristles on all surfaces of the tail except the bottom.

The opossum has five toes on each of its feet and is plantigrade—that is, it walks on the entire foot like a bear or man, registering all of the toes and footpads in its tracks. The five toes on the front feet are narrow, and when widely spread will cover about 165°. The inside toe, corresponding

17

to the thumb, can be spread slightly wider than the others and can function as a thumb.

The hind foot of the opossum is of tremendous interest because there are four fingers and a definite thumb. It closely resembles the human hand when the thumb is held as far from the fingers as possible. It is an opposable thumb like a human thumb—that is, with its tip the animal can touch the tips of the other toes—and is a great aid to the opossum when it climbs on thin branches or picks up something. There are nonretractable nails on all of the toes except the thumb.

The opossum does a lot of "grinning," displaying all of its teeth. This "grin" seems to be a snarl or grimace that is used as a visual warning to other animals to keep their

The right hind foot of an opossum. Note the "thumb" that is like a human thumb, and nails on the other toes.

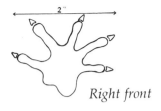
Right front

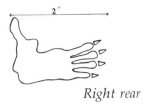
Right rear

distance. The opossum has quite a mouthful of teeth to display—50 of them, which is more than any other North American mammal. There are 18 incisors, 4 canines, 12 premolars, and 16 molars. The canine teeth are long, sharp, and slightly rear-curving. The molars have sharp points.

I have observed opossums for many years and have noticed that they don't necessarily follow trails. An opossum wanders aimlessly about an open space, content to eat whatever it encounters that is edible. Also they don't exhibit fear as do other animals. I've often walked right up to an opossum with it acting totally unconcerned. Any other animal would have vanished as quickly as possible. For these and other reasons I have always claimed that the opossum just had to be the most stupid animal roaming the face of the earth. It will step into a bare trap that almost every other animal will avoid. The opossum doesn't need my concern for its intellectual capacity, however. It has been roaming this earth for a very long time and will continue to do so for a long time to come.

Vernon Baily, a naturalist with the U.S. Biological Survey, was interested in the opossum's brain case. The larger the brain case, in relation to the total body size, the more intelligence the creature has. He found that the opossum's

brain case held 25 dried beans while a raccoon's brain case held 150 dried beans. William Hamilton made similar studies, but he used the skull of a house cat because the two animals are closer in size and weight. The house cat's brain case held 125 beans to the opossum's 25. However, the opossum has been here on earth a lot longer than either the raccoon or the house cat.

The question I seek to answer is, why has this animal been around so long? The answer has to be its adaptability and its ability to reproduce. The opossum will feed on anything dead or alive, so it seldom starves unless there is a prolonged period of very cold weather in which it cannot hunt. It also has two or even three broods of 8 to 10 young a year. These characteristics have enabled it to thrive while other more intelligent animals have become extinct.

The opossum "grins" and bares its teeth as a warning to other animals. The tail can be used for grasping.

3

Where to Find an Opossum

The generally moderating temperatures of the last century in North America have allowed many birds, animals, and even plants to expand their range northward. The opossum was primarily a southern animal until the late 1890s, and then it started north. It is now found from the border of Old Mexico to southern Ontario in Canada, from the plains states to the Atlantic Ocean. It was introduced into California about 1910 and has since spread northward along the coastal regions of Oregon and Washington into British Columbia. Rare in some of the Western states, the opossum is listed as being absent from Nevada, Utah, Idaho, and Montana, and also from North Dakota.

The opossum was found in the Palisades area of New Jersey in 1895 and in the Hudson Valley in early 1900. The first New Hampshire record is 1915, and it was first seen in Connecticut in 1927. It was scarce in the southern tier of New York counties until 1925, and a friend told me he

OPOSSUM
(Didelphis marsupialis)
CURRENT RANGE

caught the first opossum in northwestern New Jersey, my home area, in 1928. Opossums were in northern New York in 1953 and crossed into Canada shortly thereafter.

The opossum is a constant traveler, although it does its traveling over a comparatively small area. With the exception of the winter den, and the female's use of a den while she has her young, the opossum seems to end up at a different location in its range each morning.

One of the methods used today to study the range of an animal—the area of land it uses during its lifetime to survive—is live trapping. By this method, an animal is trapped, marked, and the location of its trapping noted. If the same animal is trapped or spotted by an observer in another area, this is also noted. After a period of time, all the sightings and trapping locations are noted on a map, and a general idea of the animal's range can be determined. In the case of opossums, this is a most effective method, and has shown that their home range is about fifty acres.

The opossum is not territorial, and individual ranges often overlap. "Territorial" means that an animal or bird has an area that it considers exclusively its own, and defends it against any intrusion from another animal or bird of the same species. Foxes and robins are territorial, as are many other animals. However, it has been figured that there are some twenty opossums to a square mile and the greatest distance one might travel from its point of release after trapping is seven miles.

An exception to the opossum's constant traveling is a dependable food source. When grapes or persimmons are

24

ripe, an opossum will stay in the area until the food is depleted. I have had opossums visit my bird feeding station consistently, night after night, to eat the grain or food scraps that I put out for them. When coming to a feeding station, they become very punctual, arriving each night within a few minutes of their regular time.

Opossums usually walk very deliberately, carefully searching the ground for anything edible. They are con-

The opossum spends more time traveling around than it does in a den.

stantly snuffling under the leaves for insects, nuts, or fruit, under rotted pieces of wood for grubs. They meander; they usually don't follow footpaths, trails, and roads but cross and recross and then cross again the terrain they are vacuuming.

If disturbed, the opossum runs off in what can only be called a very fast walk. As it waddles off at its fastest speed, its tail moves from side to side to help it keep its balance. Because the opossum is built so low to the ground, it can go under bushes, brush, all types of vegetation that become obstacles to its pursuer.

It is amazing how such a slow animal can so often get away. The opossum will seek refuge in the first hole in the ground or crevasse in the rocks it comes to. It can climb well but seems to do so only as a last resort. The tree it climbs may be just a sapling, which will get the opossum out of the reach of a dog but from which it can be plucked by a man. The opossum is a good swimmer and can escape by taking to the water. Recent research has shown that the opossum, although primarily a forest animal, is seldom found beyond 750 yards from water of some sort. It has now been learned that the opossum also frequents water to search for food.

Opossums may scurry up a sapling to get out of reach of a dog.

4

What an Opossum Eats

I have caught opossums near streams, but for a long time did not know that one of their favorite foods was crayfish. It had never been recorded, but then I observed them actually catching and eating this small freshwater crustacean. I did know that they frequently scavenged the dead shad that litter the Delaware River bank after the spawning season is over.

In less than a hundred years the opossum has extended its habitat over most of the United States and into Canada. One of the major reasons is its fantastic population explosion. And one reason for a population explosion is its dietary habits. If anything is edible, the opossum eats it. I am going to list foods it eats in the order of importance.

Insects lead the list. Insects are exceedingly numerous during the warm months, are easy to catch, and are a rich source of protein. Crickets and grasshoppers are examples. Fruits of all kinds are eaten. The opossum either picks up the fruits and berries that have fallen from the tree or simply climbs up after them. It is able to get near fruit on a tree that is inaccessible to other animals. Deer can reach only so high on a tree or bush, and raccoons are often too heavy to reach the ends of thin branches. The opossum can use its tail as it swings down to reach the fruit.

All types of invertebrates—creatures lacking a spinal column, such as crayfish, snails, and earthworms—are consumed. Crayfish can be difficult to catch, but the snails and earthworms are there for the picking up. On rainy nights, large numbers of earthworms swarm out of the soil and opossums can be seen filling their bellies with these muddy delicacies.

The opossum is usually too slow to catch an adult rabbit or even a full-grown mouse. Yet, with its constant snooping around and aided by the law of averages, the opossum uncovers the nests of young rabbits and mice. And the opossum would not hesitate to attack an adult rabbit if it had the chance. Frogs, salamanders, and the smaller snakes are easier to catch and are eaten. Grain is not as important to the opossum as it is to the raccoon. It is not a major food but an important incidental.

Research has shown that ground-nesting birds and their eggs and, to a lesser extent, tree-nesting birds, provide a very small part of the opossum's diet. The opossum's appearance in my area, years ago, preceded a tremendous decline in the population of the ruffed grouse. The winters were very harsh in 1977, 1978, and 1979, which caused the opossum population a temporary setback in the northeastern section of the country. I am anxious to see if there is a corresponding upswing in the ruffed grouse population. I am fully aware of the grouse's cycle and other factors involved, but I am watching to see if the decline in opossum numbers will help the grouse.

All meat-eaters feed upon whatever deer carcasses can be found in the woods, and the opossum is no exception. Evidence of small game animals and birds always appears in the opossum's feces or stomach studies as soon as the hunting season begins. This is game that has been shot at and wounded but never recovered by the two-legged hunters. Many wounded creatures crawl into an underground burrow and, if that burrow happens to be inhabited by an opossum, the situation is similar to having your groceries delivered. Even if the burrow is uninhabited, opossums will almost surely check it out as they pass by. Opossums are killed on the highways so frequently because they are often attracted to the road by some other animal having been killed there.

Cannibalism is common with opossums. I cannot say that an opossum will kill another to eat it, but I have seen them feed on the carcasses of their own kind that had been killed. I first saw this as a young boy on our family farm. One evening I skinned out several opossums and went out in the darkness to hang them in an old cherry tree. As I shone the flashlight on the tree, I was amazed to see a huge male opossum eating one of the carcasses I had previously hung there.

Opossums, although not as clever about getting into a

An opossum is constantly searching for food. It can get to fruit on thin tree branches that heavier animals cannot reach.

garbage can as a raccoon, will do it. They will go anywhere food scraps are available.

The opossum's sense of smell is highly developed and is its most important sense. It is always sniffing and snuffling as it walks along, gleaning every particle that is edible. I have often watched an opossum raise its head to sniff the air as if for potential danger. But I get the impression that the message isn't getting through. The opossum apparently depends on its nose primarily for food-gathering, but depends on its ears to warn it of danger. Most of the opossum's moves, when confronted with danger, seem to be reaction, not direct action as would be the case if it had forewarning.

The opossum's eyes are large for its body size, as befits a nocturnal animal. Its night vision is very good. Its eyes are probably not good for distance, but they are not needed for that.

Being omnivorous—eating anything, animal or vegetable—the opossum probably does not have a highly developed sense of taste. It does have food preferences, but it can eat an American toad whose skin secretions would sicken a dog.

The opossum is remarkably free of ectoparasites—creatures such as lice that live on the outside of an animal. There are several reasons for this. The opossum is solitary and parasites thrive when animals congregate. Most opossums use a different den site every day and so the den does not become infested. Opossums are subject to chiggers and ticks and, to a much lesser extent, fleas. They are also plagued with intestinal parasites such as roundworms, flatworms, and tapeworms.

5

Baby Opossums

Opossums are solitary animals except for their brief time of mating and for the time when the mother is carrying her young. They do not mate for life. Males will breed with every available female.

Usually there are two litters a year. Dr. Carl Hartman, zoologist and former professor at the University of Texas, claimed that the opossums in south Texas occasionally had three litters per year. But there is very little evidence of that occurring, and over most of their range there are two annual litters. In the opossum's most northern range it may have only a single litter.

The breeding season extends from January (in the south) or February (in the north) to August. There are peaks in the season, with the majority of opossums mating in mid-February and in June. Young opossums do not breed in the same year they are born, but are capable of breeding when they are six to eight months old.

A mother opossum and young

Opossums have a short gestation period, the time of development inside the mother before the young are born. Baby opossums are born just thirteen days after conception. They finish their development in the pouch on the mother's abdomen.

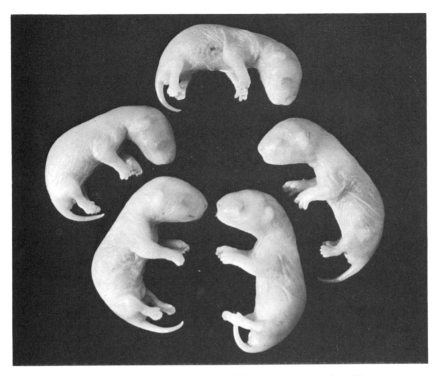

Opossums are incredibly tiny at birth. These are two weeks old.

At birth opossums are blind and naked and incredibly small, no larger than a honeybee. They weigh only 0.16 of a gram. It takes twenty-three of them to equal the weight of a penny. The newborn young has no ears, the eyes are dark spots seen through the skin, the hind feet are only little clubs, the tail a stub. The front feet, however, are fully developed and able to propel the tiny opossum upward fairly rapidly to the mother's pouch. Once she has licked it free of liquid, it climbs "hand over hand" into the pouch, a distance of three to four inches. Opossum babies have been timed at making the trip in less than a minute.

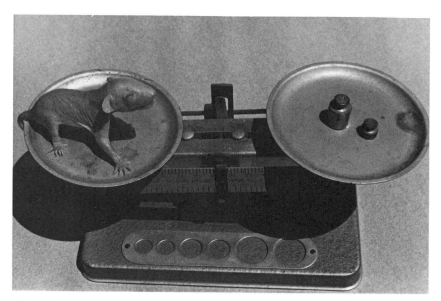

At eight weeks, an opossum weighs only about 12 grams and is just a couple of inches long, not counting the tail.

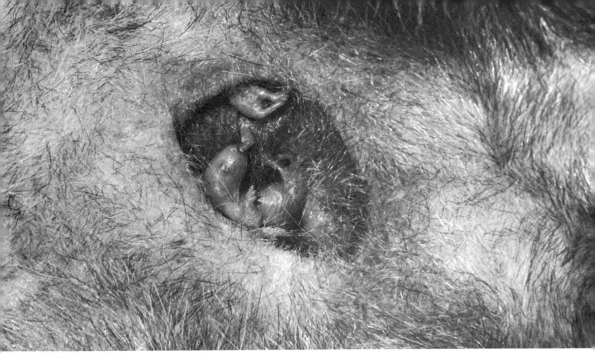

Baby opossums in mother's pouch

The mother's pouch is where the baby will be warmed, fed, and protected for the next 80 to nearly 90 days. It has a rim that is controlled by muscles that allow it to be relaxed and open or tightened and closed. The pouch stretches greatly as the young grow. Inside the pouch the female

Opossum's pouch closed

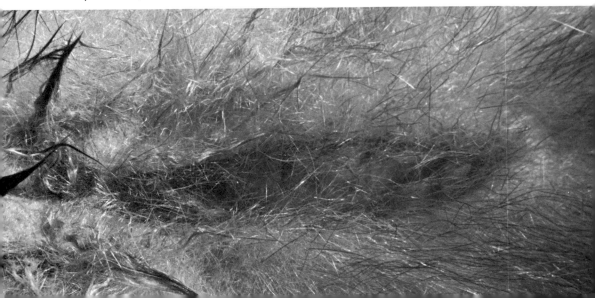

usually has twelve nipples arranged in an inverted U-shape with a thirteenth nipple in the center. Opossums have been found with as few as nine nipples and as many as seventeen, but thirteen is normal.

As each baby enters the pouch it seeks out a nipple and swallows it. The nipple then expands to fill its mouth and throat, effectively fastening it in place in the pouch. Once secured, the young opossum does not let go of the nipple for six to seven weeks and can only be removed with great effort. If there are more young born than there are nipples to accommodate them, they are ejected from the pouch.

The opossum's pouch is an efficient incubator. The young nurse; the milk is not pumped by the mother as was believed earlier. The female cleans out voided material, but the pouch becomes stained. At two weeks the sex of the babies can be determined. Shortly after, the hair covering begins to push through the skin. The young are able to open their mouths between the 42nd and 49th days. Their eyes open between the 58th and 72nd days. The young stay in the pouch until between the 80th and 87th day.

Several years ago I raised three families of opossums and learned many fascinating things. During the time when the young were older than sixty days, they would often come out of the mother's pouch, although they remained fastened to her nipples. They would hang backwards out of her pouch as she lay on her side. If she were disturbed, the

Fifteen-day-old opossums fastened to teats in mother's pouch

39

Baby opossums nursing

little ones would scramble back inside, and sometimes they had trouble fitting. Sometimes the mother would climb into her nest box dragging some of the young behind her. I never did see one come loose.

After the 80th day, the young release their holds on their mother's nipples and begin to venture out of the pouch.

Drawings and paintings frequently show the mother opossum going about with her tail bent up over her back with all of her babies hanging by their tails wrapped around hers. However, I have never seen this occurring.

The baby opossums do ride around hanging onto their mother's back, their tiny paws clutching her hair. There are often too many babies to be taken on one ride, and some will be left back at the den. Their combined weights are a great handicap when the mother goes foraging for food.

The young are weaned between the 95th and 100th day

Mother opossum with young about seven weeks old

and are no longer dependent on the mother's milk. After that time, if a baby falls off when the mother goes out with them, it doesn't matter. At this age, the little ones are big enough and strong enough to go off on their own. If the young are born in February, most of them are gone from the den by the middle of May. The female is ready for mating again and the next litter is born in mid-June. As soon as the female is bred again, her nipples, which have been stretched to as much as one and a half inches in length as the babies nursed, shrink drastically so that they will be small enough for her next litter to get in their tiny mouths.

During the days and nights from the 80th to the 100th day, the little opossum learns from its mother the habits that will ensure its survival. It learns to forage for food, about its natural enemies, how to hide and climb as defense, and how to fight, though an opossum would rather run than fight. The young are never very far from their place of birth. They disperse on an average of about 400 yards from the den where they were born.

The life span for the opossum is five to seven years. In protected areas, many live to be five years old. The oldest opossum on record was a captive one that lived to be eight years old.

Mother opossum with young clinging to her hair

Three-month-old baby opossums

6

Opossum Behavior

Everyone knows that the opossum is famous for "playing possum." This bit of information is the one "fact" that most people know about the opossum. It does happen but, in my experience observing opossums, it does not happen all that often.

What actually occurs when this situation takes place is that the opossum falls over on its side, its mouth gapes open, and saliva drools out of its mouth. The front feet are clutched into balls and the body becomes limp. In this state the opossum can be picked up, poked, prodded, shaken, or bitten by a dog without giving any sign of life. A breath rate is difficult to discern, as is a heartbeat. If the opossum is left alone and thinks the danger has passed, it soon arises, looks around, and runs as fast as it can. Opossums have a tremendous tenacity for life.

The chances of seeing an opossum "playing possum" are almost nil at night. It is usually seen when the opossum is caught out during daylight hours and threatened with

An opossum "playing possum"

danger. Under cover of darkness, when the opossum is in its element, it is usually able to make good its escape or, if cornered, it is more apt to put up a fight. The opossum is no coward, especially for an animal that weighs only four to eight pounds.

When the opossum stands its ground, it raises up as high as it can on all four legs, holds its tail straight up over its back and, with widely gaping jaws, faces its enemy. I have seen opossums bluff much larger raccoons away from food at the feeder. I am not saying that opossums are fighters, but at times they are certainly willing to stand their ground and display fierceness.

Opossums are very clean animals. They spend a lot of time grooming themselves, washing themselves with their tongues like a cat. When feeding, I have observed them spend as much as twenty minutes washing their forepaws with their tongues, then wetting their forepaws and thoroughly scrubbing their faces. They often sit upright and groom their bodies.

I have watched these animals at my feeder eating fatty meat scraps. They will eat, then stop and wash themselves, and eat some more, then wash again. I have always wondered why they don't wait until they have finished eating to wash, but they don't and I still don't have the answer.

Opossums are amazingly quiet animals. They are not as vocal as are many others, which leads me to believe that much of their communication is accomplished through their keen sense of smell. Perhaps their odors convey meanings to other opossums. I do know that they purr to their young and growl and hiss when angry.

The most commonly heard sound is their loud hissing when they are angry. I have also heard them growl when threatened. Their wide, gaping mouths and sharp teeth help frighten enemies. Opossums at my feeder gape and charge at one another, but usually the gape is enough to make a lesser opossum defer to the larger.

Opossums will void their feces at the bases of large trees in their areas. I do not know if this is merely their toilet station or if they are claiming that particular parcel of turf.

Another thing people "know" about opossums is that they hang by their tails. This is not exactly true. I've observed opossums for many years and I've never seen an adult one hang by its tail. It is true that the opossum uses

An opossum about six weeks old hanging by its tail and a foot.

An opossum can hang by its tail, but an adult one usually needs support from its feet.

50

its tail as a fifth hand when it climbs, or as a brake when it descends a tree headfirst. And it does hold on with its tail when it climbs from one branch to another. A young opossum can support its body weight with its tail for a considerable period of time, but an adult cannot. The tail soon loses its grip and the opossum is on its way down.

The tail is used by the opossum to carry things, particularly litter. When the opossum moves into a den or is refurbishing the one it is using, it will carry lots of leaves and litter into the den with its tail. It gathers leaves together with its front feet, passes them back to its hind feet which

Baby opossums in a hollow of a tree

push them back to where they are looped up by the tail rolling down and forward. With its load secure, the opossum takes its bedding home.

Underground dens are preferred by the opossum and where these are scarce it will use a hollow tree, or take over a squirrel's leafy nest, adding lots more leaves to the original nest. If there are no holes, hollow trees, or nests, this very adaptable creature will find shelter wherever it can. In populated areas, opossums have been known to den under porches, in garages, in storm sewers, or any other conceivable spot that could be considered a shelter.

7

Survival in Winter

Opossums are almost strictly nocturnal during the warmer periods of the year. During the winter, when they are very hungry, they will forage during the daylight hours. When the weather is moderate, I have found that the opossums come to my feeder about 8:30 P.M., never while it is light.

Different animals deal with the cold of winter in different ways. Some migrate, moving to a warmer climate. Some hibernate, going into a deep sleep with the heartbeat slowed down and the body temperature drastically dropped. They don't need to eat or drink for up to three months. Others just cope with the weather, and the opossum is one of these. It has always been a southern animal, its range extending northward because of a generally moderating climate. It does not migrate or hibernate. It cannot even spend extended periods of time in its den as does the raccoon or skunk. A warm-climate animal is patterned to leave its den and forage.

53

Opossums do gorge themselves in autumn, becoming very fat before the onset of winter. I have seen fat layers an inch in depth beneath the skin. One large male possum that was live-trapped in early December was found to have lost 50 percent of his body weight when retrapped the following spring.

During the most bitter weather the opossum stays in its den for as long a period as possible. Females will stay in their dens longer than males, but neither can remain long enough to escape winter's cold. If the cold is protracted, lasting two weeks or longer, the opossum must come out to seek food.

But opossums are not really suited for winter foraging. The bottoms of their feet are bare, the ears are naked, and the tail sports only a few bristly hairs. Their tail tips and ear tips invariably freeze off. Both appendages may lose additional portions on succeeding jaunts. The opossum does not seem to be handicapped by this loss. It seems to have little or no effect on them. No infection takes place because of the freezing. Occasionally there is self-mutilation of tail tips by opossums in captivity, probably because of nervousness.

If the winter is a long one, many opossums die of starvation. Our recent hard winters have been a great setback to the opossums in the Northeast. When thaws occur in January or February, you will see tremendous opossum activity as they scramble about searching for food.

8

Opossums and People

How do we know that a nocturnal animal has been in an area? The answer is signs. Signs are just what the word implies: marks, tracks, and droppings an animal leaves behind whenever it moves through an area.

There can be no mistaking the opossum's tracks for those of any other animal. It is the only animal in North America that makes a distinctly separate and clawless "thumb" print with its rear feet. The tracks can be seen in the mud around pond and stream edges, and are often seen in a wandering pattern through the snow. Another telltale sign that the tracks are opossum is the fact that they never go in a single direction, unless the opossum is being pursued.

Except for the places it uses as toilet stations, its feces are seldom seen. The most common sign of the opossum are their dead bodies lying along roads. Where they are plentiful, more opossums are killed by automobiles than any other animal. When opossums wander onto a highway,

Opossum tracks are distinctive.

they most often just stand there and stare at the onrushing automobile, mesmerized. Many make no move to get out of the road, and opossums are killed by the hundreds of thousands each year.

I have found that slowing the car, blinking the lights from low to high beam again and again, and beeping the horn repeatedly often causes the opossum to move from the road, but not always. Sometimes I am forced to drive around them as they stand and stare at me.

The automobile has to be considered the opossum's number one enemy. Man and his dogs would be next. Oddly enough, the opossum does not have too many natural enemies because few animals will eat an opossum unless they are starving. The reason for this is not known. Some researchers list the red fox as eating the opossum. I don't say this doesn't happen, but I've never known of it happening. In my area of northwest New Jersey, even vultures don't eat opossums. I have deliberately placed opossum carcasses out in fields where they could easily be seen by vultures, but it is always a waste of time. I have seen vultures in Florida eat opossums, but not in my home area. Dogs will kill opossums, but I have never known one to eat one. Great horned owls are reported to kill and eat opossums, but even the owl much prefers a skunk.

Most people are turned off by the opossum's similarity in appearance to that of a big rat. Actually, I think they are a most attractive, clean, and interesting animal. They sure are different! When obtained young, some opossums become very tame, although I have never had any that I could consider a pet.

A baby opossum about six weeks old

Whatever man's opinion of this odd little marsupial may be, one thing is certain. It has been around for millions of years and will probably survive till the end of time. It was here long before man was, and will likely be here long after we have gone.

For many years the fur of the opossum was used to trim inexpensive garments. But in recent years the fur of the opossum has been so low in value that it hardly paid to skin them. According to figures of the International Association of Fish and Game Agencies, 1,064,725 opossums were sold in the United States in 1976–77 at an average price of $2.50. But many states do not keep any records of the number of opossums taken.

Opossum pelts were sent to Europe in the eighteenth and nineteenth centuries for use as decorative furs. They

Opossum up a tree

were never very popular because of their poor quality. However, with advanced techniques in the fur industry and the increased demand for fur in the twentieth century, opossum pelts became more desirable. They could be made to look like rarer and more durable fur through dressing and dyeing. With the guard hairs removed, they resemble mink. With the guard hairs retained, a silver fox simulation is possible.

For years the opossum was the poor man's chicken, particularly in the South during hard times. Opossums were plentiful and easily hunted. Even today you can find recipes for cooking opossum and people who relish possum and sweet potatoes as a tasty dish.

There is an organization called the Possum Growers and Breeders Association of America, whose president, Frank S. Clark of Clauton, Alabama, is promoting the increased use of opossum as food. Their slogan is "Eat More Possum."

Index

LEONARD LEE RUE III has devoted his life to photographing and writing about wildlife. Today he is the most widely published wildlife photographer in North America and probably the world. His work appears in over fifty publications a month here and abroad.

His most recent book is *The Deer of North America*. For young readers he has covered the red fox, white-tailed deer, beaver, and ruffed grouse. Rue is a former camp ranger, wilderness canoe guide, and game keeper. He lectures to school and civic groups and conducts outdoor educational field trips.

WILLIAM OWEN, a close friend of the author, is a Presbyterian minister in Frenchtown, New Jersey. He has long been interested in wildlife and is co-author of *The Search* with Tom Brown, Jr., the story of Brown's experience as a woodsman and tracker, and of wilderness survival.